Larry Wilde is an American from New Jersey. He served in the United States Marine Corps and graduated from the University of Miami, Florida. Mr Wilde entertains at leading hotels and nightclubs in the United States and is the author of two previous works dealing with comedy techniques: *The Great Comedians* and *How the Great Comedy Writers Create Laughter*.

Also in this series:

THE OFFICIAL IRISH JOKE BOOK

THE OFFICIAL IRISH JOKE BOOK NO 3 (Book 2 to follow)

THE OFFICIAL SCOTTISH JOKE BOOK

THE WORLD'S WORST JOKE BOOK

THE OFFICIAL AUSSIE JOKE BOOK

POSITIVELY THE LAST IRISH JOKE BOOK

THE OFFICIAL IRISH JOKE BOOK NO 4

THE OFFICIAL ANGLER'S JOKE BOOK

DELAYED BY FOG IN TIMBUCTOO

THE OFFICIAL CAT LOVERS/DOG LOVERS JOKE BOOK

Larry Wilde

The Official
Jewish Joke Book

Futura Publications Limited

A Futura Book

First published in Great Britain by
Futura Publications Limited in 1980

ISBN 0 7088 1849 8

Made and printed in Great Britain by
Hazell Watson & Viney Ltd
Aylesbury, Bucks

Futura Publications Limited
110 Warner Road,
Camberwell, London SE5

This book is dedicated to Milton Josefsberg, my friend, my golf partner, and my tutor, with grateful appreciation, to Gertie and Selig, who made it all possible and for beautiful Aunt Bella – a gray-haired Jewish lady with sparkling Irish eyes and a heart full of love for all humanity.

SHALOM

Out of the Middle East conflicts have come much heartbreak and tragedy—and comedy. Despite the bloodshed and bitter desert warfare, Israel managed a smile. Here are some of the classic lines that turned tears to laughter:

After fighting only twenty-four hours, the Israelis released the following communiqué:
TODAY WE DOWNED 900 PLANES. 600 DEFINITE. 300 PLEDGED.

* * *

ISRAELI ENLISTMENT POSTER
Join the Army and See the Pyramids

* * *

An Israeli soldier apologized for capturing only 8 tanks and 250 prisoners. "After all, my husband wasn't with me!"

Two foot soldiers in Jerusalem were talking over a glass of tea.

"What's our goal today?"

"We capture the Suez Canal!"

"Good! But what'll we do in the afternoon?"

* * *

How do you know an Egyptian flag when you see it?

It's all white!

* * *

WORLD'S THINNEST BOOK
Arab Military Victories

* * *

Israeli Intelligence has discovered a key Egyptian military photo. It's a picture of the Arabs practicing war maneuvers— throwing their hands up in the air.

* * *

At one point in the campaign, an Arab division spotted a lone Israeli sniper on a sand dune. The commander dispatched three men to get him. When they didn't return, he sent a dozen. None of them came back. Finally he sent an entire company.

Two hours later, one blood-splattered Egyptian soldier crawled back. "It was an ambush," he muttered. "There were *two* of them!"

* * *

"I th-th-think the Israelis sh-sh-should g-g-give b-b-back all the Arab t-t-territory and g-g-get the hell out of E-g-g-gypt!"

"Sure, that's easy for you to say!"

* * *

Egyptian President Sadat made a brief appearance on the Cairo television show "Where's My Line?"

* * *

Ralph Nader has launched a campaign to provide Arab tanks with back-up lights.

* * *

"It's unfair," said a U.A.R. spokesman, "Israel has two million three hundred thousand Jews on her side. And we have none!"

7

Reports from the second day of fighting indicated that the Egyptians had destroyed four Jeeps, a kosher mobile kitchen, and fourteen air-conditioned Cadillacs.

The Israelis claimed four hundred MIGs and twenty-four flying carpets.

In Jerusalem two elderly men were sitting on a park bench discussing the war.

"How long do you think it will last?"

"Two months, the most!"

"So quick?"

"My son joined the Army and he never yet held a job for longer than two months in his life!"

*　　*　　*

SIGN IN ISRAELI BARRACKS
*Privates Will Kindly Refrain from
Giving Advice to Officers.*

*　　*　　*

The air-raid siren went off in Haifa. A woman rushed down the stairs toward the basement. Suddenly she noticed that her husband had not followed her down. "Come on, Sidney," she yelled.

"Just a minute!" answered her husband. "I gotta get my teeth!"

"Never mind your teeth!" the wife shouted back. "What do you think they're dropping—pastrami sandwiches?"

*　　*　　*

A U.N. observer began chatting with an Israeli paratrooper. "How many successful jumps have you made?" asked the United Nations guard.

"Every one of the jumps was successful," said the Israeli. "I'm here!"

Yarkoni and Danberg, two Israeli soldiers, were bemoaning the years of hardship and fighting against the Egyptians.

"What we should do," suggested Yarkoni "is declare war against the United States. They'll beat us, and like they always do with all the countries they defeat, right away they'll give us billions of dollars, plenty of food, houses, cars, and factories."

"That's no good," sighed Danberg. "With our luck, *we'd* win!"

* * *

First Israeli soldier: Don't worry, God will arrange it that Sadat will die on a Jewish holiday.
Second Israeli soldier: How can you be sure?
First Israeli soldier: Listen, any day that Sadat dies will be a Jewish holiday.

* * *

Moshe Dayan can't give back the captured Arab territories—they're all in his wife's name.

A group of American tourists was being shown around Tel Aviv. They arrived at the tomb of the Unknown Soldier. The guide pointed out the inscription at the bottom of the tomb:

HERE LIES ABRAHAM SCHWARTZ. BORN 1923. DIED 1973, DURING ARAB-ISRAELI WAR. A GOOD SOLDIER AND A GREAT FURRIER.

"What's all that fur business?" asked a surprised tourist. "This is supposed to be an unknown soldier."

"That's true," said the guide. "As a soldier nobody knew him, but as a furrier he was famous!"

*   *   *

Master storyteller Myron Cohen broke up "The Tonight Show" with this gem:

Vice-President Ford arrived in Israel and asked to see the Wailing Wall. Prime Minister Meir took him to the Wall, whereupon the Vice-President began to pray.

"Help Mr. Nixon guide our country!" He turned to Mrs. Meir and asked, "Is that nice?"

"That's nice!" she answered.

"Thank you for making me the Vice-President," he directed to the Wall. And then to the Prime Minister, "Is that nice?"

"That's nice," she replied.

"Let Israel give back the land they took from the Arabs so there will be peace in the Middle East . . . Is that nice?"

"You're talking to a wall!" said Mrs. Meir.

The following conversation was alleged to have taken place between the President of the United States and the Prime Minister of Israel:

Nixon: You have no idea how tough it is being President in a country with two hundred million citizens.

Meir: It's even tougher being a citizen in a country with two million Prime Ministers.

*   *   *

Kadish, a new immigrant to Israel, went to see the head of a government department for a job.

"What's your experience?" the official asked. "What can you do?"

"Nothing!" answered Kadish.

"Good!" said the civil servant. "Then we won't have to break you in!"

*   *   *

"Are there any golf courses in Israel?" asked a tourist of his guide.

"Think about it," his guide replied. "In a country as tiny as ours, a good drive could become an international incident!"

*   *   *

What's the fastest thing on earth?

An Arab riding a bicycle down Collins Avenue in Miami Beach.

Teitelbaum was taking his first jet plane ride. Nervous and on the verge of nausea, he had just buckled his seat belt when a huge Arab with long flowing robes sat down beside him.

After takeoff, the Arab immediately fell asleep and Teitelbaum yearned to visit the lavatory. He feared waking the sleeping giant beside him. Finally, Teitelbaum became so sick to his stomach that he threw up all over the Arab's beautiful robes.

Ten minutes later, the Arab awoke and was shocked to see the mess on his clothes. Teitelbaum smiled at him and said, "You feel better now?"

Overheard in New York's Garment District:

"I'm in favor of putting a statue of Sadat in the middle of Times Square."

"For what?"

"It'll give us shade in the summertime, shelter in the wintertime, and the birds a chance to speak for us all."

*   *   *

Rabbi Jacob Pressman of Temple Beth Am in Los Angeles tells about the French, English, and Israeli archeologists captured by two Arabs in the Sinai Desert.

"You dogs! We're going to kill you!"

"Vive la France!" shouted the Frenchman. "I'm ready!"

"God save the Queen!" proclaimed the Englishman. "Go ahead and shoot!"

"Punch me in the nose first!" begged the Israeli. And the Arabs pummeled him.

"Kick me in the behind!" said the Israeli.

"With pleasure!" answered the Arabs. And they did so with great relish.

"Now," said the Israeli, "hit me in the stomach!"

The Arabs pounded him to the ground. The Israeli then pulled out a gun and shot both Arabs dead.

"That was wonderful!" said the Englishman. "But why did you allow them to beat you so unmercifully?"

"If I'd shot them first," said the Israeli, "I would've been condemned as the aggressor!"

Prime Minister Indira Gandhi visited Israel and was welcomed by Golda Meir. After seeing all the historical sights, Mrs. Gandhi said, "I would like to visit a synagogue!"

"By all means!" answered the Israeli Prime Minister.

Two weeks later, Mrs. Gandhi stood before her Cabinet. "What did you learn in Israel?" asked one of the members.

"Many things!" answered the Indian Prime Minister. "But most of all I learned that in Israel synagogues, the men pray on the first floor and the Prime Ministers worship in the balcony!"

*   *   *

Two men meet in Palestine.
"Say, aren't you from New York?"
"Yes!"
"What's your name?"
"Riley!"
"*Riley?* What are you doing over here?"
"Living the life of Cohen!"

*   *   *

"Me, I blame everything on Moses!"

"What does he have to do with our troubles?"

"When Moses crossed the Red Sea, if he'd a made a left turn instead of a right, the Arabs would've gotten the sand and we would've gotten the oil."

George Jessel, renowned for his eulogies at funerals, was once ribbed by Jack Benny at a Friar's Roast:

"One of the nicest eulogies I ever heard Jessel deliver was for one of James Mason's cats. You just wouldn't believe what that cat had done for Israel!"

* * *

Ten minutes after the El Al jet left the Tel Aviv airport, a voice came over the loudspeaker:

"Good evening, this is your captain. I wanna wish you all a wonderful trip. God willing, we'll get you there safely. But God forbid we do have trouble, you'll find life belts under your seats. And if you have to put them on, God help us, you should wear them in the best of health!"

* * *

Milton Wildman, New Jersey stock market analyst, returned from a visit to Israel with this classic contribution:

Mrs. Lupowitz, an elderly widow newly arrived in the Holy Land, jumped into a public taxi traveling from Tel Aviv to Haifa. To the annoyance of the other five passengers, she kept reminding the driver, "Tell me when we pass Shefayim!"

Mrs. Lupowitz asked the driver so many times that the poor man drove right through Shefayim. When he realized his mistake, he apologized to the other occupants, turned the vehicle around, and drove back.

"Here is Shefayim!" said the driver. "Now you can get out!"

"Who wants to get out!" said Mrs. Lupowitz.

"You did!"

"No," said Mrs. Lupowitz. "My daughter told me when I left Tel Aviv that when I pass Shefayim, I should take my medicine."

*　　*　　*

SHMALTZ

Roses are red,
Violets are bluish.
If it wasn't for Christmas,
We'd all be Jewish.

*   *   *

Weinberg came home unexpectedly and found Mrs. Weinberg in bed with another man. "What the hell are you doing?" shouted the irate husband.

"See?" said his wife to the man beside her. "Didn't I tell you he was stupid?"

*   *   *

How can you tell the difference between a Jew and an Italian?
The Jew is the one in the Italian suit.

Paul Mosher, TV promotional giveaway king, got howls at a friend's dinner party with this switch on married life:

Mr. and Mrs. Blumstein stood outside the gorilla cage at the zoo. They gaped at the huge animal for a long time, unaware that the ape was staring at Mrs. Blumstein and becoming sexually aroused.

Suddenly, it became apparent that the gorilla had an erection. He reached through the bars, pulled Mrs. Blumstein into the cage, and began ripping off her clothes. "What should I do?" she screamed hysterically to her husband.

"Do what you do with me," replied Mr. Blumstein. "Tell him you got a headache!"

Newman went to Florida for his health, and two weeks later died of a heart attack. His body was shipped back to New York for the funeral. Two of Newman's friends came to see him as he lay in the casket.

"Doesn't he look wonderful?" said the first.

"Yeah," said the other. "Those two weeks in Florida sure did him a world of good!"

*   *   *

Rubin and Marcus, who were gin-rummy addicts, met one day in the country-club card room. Rubin had just learned that Marcus had been making love to his spouse.

"Look," said Rubin, "I know you've been foolin' around with my wife, but I still love her. So let's settle this in a civilized way."

"What do you want to do?" asked Marcus.

"I'll play you one game of gin; the winner gets to keep my wife!"

"Okay," agreed Marcus. "But just to make it interesting—let's play for a penny a point!"

*   *   *

JEWISH FAIRY
Heblew
24

In the state of New York, out on Long Island, there is a charming suburban town called Massapequa. There are so many Jewish and Italian residents in Massapequa that the city fathers are thinking of changing the name to Matzoh–Pizza.

* * *

Stern had just returned from a Florida vacation. "How was the weather?" asked a friend.

"It was so hot in Miami Beach," said Stern, "the women weren't wearing their mink stoles—just the appraisals!"

* * *

Mickey Katz, the ever-popular musician-comedian, fractures audiences with this one:

Silverstein, the inveterate joiner, came rushing home, proudly holding a membership card to his newest organization.

"Look," said Silverstein to his son, "I just joined the Prostitute Club!"

"What?" said the boy. "Let me see that card!" After reading it, he announced: "Pa, that's the Parachute Club!"

"All I know is," said Silverstein, "they guaranteed me three hundred sixty-five jumps a year!"

25

Mrs. Fleishman and Mrs. Rutkin were rocking on the porch of their Catskill Mountain hotel.

"Oh, my God!" exclaimed Mrs. Fleishman. "Look at that boy. Did you ever see such a big nose? Such a crooked mouth? And look—he's cockeyed too!"

"That," said Mrs. Rutkin, "happens to be my son!"

"Well," said Mrs. Fleishman, "on *him*, it's very becoming!"

* * *

Bob Mitchell, the exclusive wallpaper designer-manufacturer, tells about the Shoenfelds, who were upstairs in their bed.

"Wake up!" cried Mrs. Shoenfeld, nudging her husband. "There are burglars in the kitchen. I think they're eating the pot roast I made tonight!"

"What do we care," said Mr. Shoenfeld. "As long as they don't die in the house!"

* * *

By mistake, Rosenbloom walked into the women's locker room of an exclusive country club and started taking a shower. Suddenly, he heard female voices.

Realizing where he was, Rosenbloom wrapped a towel around his head and began walking toward the exit.

"Thank God!" gasped one lady, staring

at his nakedness intently. "It's not my husband!"

"He's not mine, either!" retorted the gal beside her.

"Girls," announced a third woman, "he's not even a member of the club!"

*   *   *

Irene Ginsburg, dynamic fund-raiser for the National Council of Jewish Women, heard this at one of her charity events:

Rosenfeld walked into the house with a grin on his face. "You'll never guess what a bargain I just got," he told his wife. "I bought four polyester, steel-belted, radial, wide-tread, whitewall, heavy-duty tires. On sale yet!"

"Are you nuts?" shrieked Mrs. Rosenfeld. "What did you buy tires for? You don't even have a car!"

"So?" said Rosenfeld. "You buy brassieres, don't you?"

*   *   *

"My name is Mortimer P. Quinn!"

"How do you spell Quinn?"

"C-o-h-e-n."

"What does the 'P' stand for?"

"The 'P' is silent, like in water!"

"There's no 'P' in water."

"I could see you was never swimming in Coney Island."

27

A German politician pleaded with Hitler not to mistreat the Jews. "If for no other reason," he said, "than just because they're so smart!"

"What makes you think the Jews are so smart?" asked the dictator.

"Come and I'll show you!"

He took the Nazi leader to Guttman's Gift Shop and said, "Ask him for a *left*-handed teapot."

The Führer did. Guttman went to the back of the store, picked up a teapot, turned it around, and returned.

"You're in luck," said Guttman, handing the teapot to Hitler. "I just happened to have one left!"

Back out on the street, the politician said, "You see, that's what I mean about the Jews being so smart!"

"What's so smart about that?" exclaimed Hitler. "He just happened to have one left!"

*   *   *

The whole world is Jewish. Even the sun is called Sol.

*   *   *

In the days of sailing ships men were often punished by whipping. And so it was that Swenson, Polski, and Rabinowitz were to be flogged for their misdeeds.

"Before I beat you," said the Captain to the Swede, "what do you want on your back?"

"I want some grease!" said Swenson.

After the flogging, the captain asked the same question of the Pole.

"I strong," said Polski. "I want nothing on my back!"

When the thirty lashes had been given, the captain said, "All right, Rabinowitz, what do you want on your back?"

"Well," said Rabinowitz, "I'd like to have that Polack on my back!"

*   *   *

Comedian Aloysius Bernie overheard this exchange in the cocktail lounge of the Concord Hotel:

Young man: Are you dancing?
Young woman: Are you asking?
Young man: I'm asking!
Young woman: I'm dancing!

*   *   *

WIFELY COMMENTS DURING LOVEMAKING WITH HUSBAND

Italian: Oh, Gino, you are the world's greatest lover!

French: Ah, Jacques, my darling, you are marvelous! More! More!

Jewish: Oy, Jake, the ceiling needs painting!

Brotsky sent his only son to Europe to study the violin. Eight years later the boy returned, and Brotsky rented Carnegie Hall for his debut.

"If my son is a big hit," said Brotsky to all his relatives and friends, "we're gonna have a celebration party in the main ballroom of the Waldorf Astoria."

The big night arrived. The boy walked out on stage and was terrible. The violin squeaked. The strings broke. The audience was bored to death.

Brotsky, realizing the night was a gigantic failure, rushed over to the Waldorf to cancel the dinner. Sitting at a front table were three relatives, eating like crazy.

"What are you doing here?" shouted Brotsky. "I told you I'd have a party only if my son was a success!"

"Whaddaya want from us?" asked a fifth cousin. "*We* liked him!"

* * *

BAGEL
A doughnut dipped in cement

* * *

"Every girl I bring home, my mother doesn't like," said Norman to an old college chum. "They're either too tall or too short, too smart or too dumb, too fat or too thin, too loud or too quiet. I just can't seem to please her!"

"Just keep looking," said his friend, "till you find a girl who looks like your mother. Then she can't find fault with her!"

Three months later, Norman met his buddy again. "I did what you said," he announced. "I looked and I looked until I finally found a girl just like my mother. The same height, the same weight, the same personality, the same mind. She was exactly like my mother!"

"What happened?"

"My father hated her!"

* * *

Sidney Stevens, of Mannis Furs at Caesar's Palace in Las Vegas, overheard this conversation:

"Whatsa matter, Harry?"

"Ah, my wife is allergic to fur. Every time she sees another woman wearing a mink coat—she gets sick!"

* * *

Seymour telephoned his mother from London. "I didn't want you to think I forgot your birthday, Mama," he said. "I'm sending you a Picasso and a Jaguar!"

Three weeks later, he called again. "Did you get the two gifts I sent you?"

"I only got one!" answered his mother.

"Which one?"

"I don't know!"

31

Nils Shapiro, New York marketing exec, saw a crowd lining Riverside Drive to cheer Cardinal Spellman. Loudest of the cheerers was a little old Jewish lady, holding her granddaughter aloft to catch a glimpse of the passing prelate.

"It's very nice of you to get so excited over Cardinal Spellman!" observed Shapiro.

"Cardinal Spellman!" repeated the startled old lady. "I thought it was Mischa Elman!"

* * *

Maury Gidlow, sales champ for Carroll & Co. in Beverly Hills, came up with this classic:

Kotch and Wexler had just finished their lunch in a Lower East Side New York restaurant. "Tea or coffee, gentlemen?" asked the waiter.

"I'll have tea!" said Kotch.

"Me too!" said Wexler. "Make sure the glass is clean!"

The waiter left and returned in a few minutes with the order. "Two teas!" he announced. "Which one asked for a clean glass?"

* * *

Two ladies met at a Hadassah luncheon. "How's your daughter?" asked Mrs. Krantz.

"Oh-h, she's married to a prince!" boasted Mrs. Gottlieb. "He lets her sleep until eleven o'clock in the morning. She doesn't have to put her fingers in cold water. And all afternoon she does nothing but sip cocktails!"

"And what about your son?" asked Mrs. Krantz.

"Oh, I'm heartbroken," moaned Mrs. Gottlieb. "That poor boy is married to such a girl—she sleeps until eleven o'clock in the morning. She doesn't lift her fingers to put them in cold water! And what do you think? She's a *drunkard!* All afternoon she does nothing but sip cocktails!"

* * *

CATSKILLS HOTEL
Little Mandy Kornblum's Chateau in the Pussy Willows

* * *

Ann Dan, Los Angeles City School Coordinator, says she's absolutely certain that during a school celebration of Christmas, one of the children sang: "God rest ye, Jerry Mendelbaum!"

* * *

Milton Blackstone, Southern California special-events producer, provides this definition of a *bris**: "It's a small surgical procedure that we Jews have turned into a catered affair."

—————————
*circumcision ceremony

The Pharaoh decided to go for a ride up the Nile. "Captain of the Guards!" he shouted. "Get eighty Jewish slaves for oarsmen!"

Two hours later, the Egyptian leader was sailing up the river. In the hold, the Jews were rowing at a wicked pace.

Lieberman, the slaves' wit, turned to the rower beside him. "Tell me," said Lieberman, "on a cruise like this, how much do you tip the whipper?"

Lee Wolfberg, talent manager and raconteur, smiles when he thinks of an aunt who lived in Brooklyn. On his way East from Hollywood, Lee sent his relative a magnum of champagne and a pound of caviar.

When he arrived in New York, he phoned her. "Did you like the gift I sent you?"

"The ginger ale wasn't so bad. But that huckleberry jelly—you must've left it standing next to some fish in the icebox all night."

* * *

Comedian Dave Barry was driving along late one night and saw a sign: MENDELSOHN'S MOTEL. Underneath, it said: TV. Dave stopped at the place, got a room, and found there was no television set.

"There's a sign outside that says 'TV,' " Barry complained to the owner.

"Naturally," said Mendelsohn. "That means, *T*ourists *V*elcome!"

* * *

Sokolow: I just got a beautiful French poodle for my wife.
Neiman: Tell me, how did you make such a good trade?

* * *

Mushkin was visiting a cemetery and noticed a magnificent marble mausoleum.

36

Above the doorway was chiseled: ROTH-SCHILD.

"Oh, boy!" said Mushkin. "Now, that's what I call living!"

* * *

Jack Lewerke, California record promoter, convulsed poker pals with this modern-day mother story:

Ira quit college, got himself a back pack, and began hitchhiking around the United States. After he had been gone more than a year, he telephoned home.

"Hello, Ma, how are you?"

"Just fine, son. When're you coming home? I'll fix you some chopped liver and chicken soup and a beautiful pot roast!"

"I'm still pretty far away!"

"Oh, son!" cried the desperate woman. "Just come home and I'll fix your favorite —oatmeal cookies!"

"I don't like oatmeal cookies!" said the boy.

"You don't?" asked the woman.

"Say," said Ira, "is this Century 5-7682?"

"No!"

"Then I must have the wrong number!"

"Does that mean you're not coming?" asked the woman.

* * *

SHTICK

Mat-zoh[1]: Temporary filling for tooth cavities.

Mish-poch-eh[2]: Foreign relations committee.

Zay-dah[3]: Grandchild's press agent.

Mach-ay-eh[4]: Finding a quarter in a phone booth.

Taka a mach-ay-eh[5]: Japanese sex relations.

Hal-vah[6]: Kasha dipped in cement.

Bar Mitzvah[7]: Jewish dude ranch.

[1]*unleavened bread* [2]*family* [3]*grandfather* [4]*good feeling* [5]*heavenly feeling* [6]*Turkish candy* [7]*ceremony held when a boy reaches the age of thirteen*

39

Far-blund-jet[8]: Owning a kosher butcher shop in Cairo.

Far-ga-nigen[9]: Front table at a nudie show.

Fay-ga-leh[10]: A man who likes to take another man to lunch and *he* is the lunch.

Yen-tah[11]: The FBI in bloomers.

Shad-chen[12]: A man who knows the perfect girl for you—and married the wrong girl himself.

Schle-miel[13]: A man who takes a bath and forgets to wash his face.

Shik-eh[14]: Jewish Dean Martin.

Shik-seh[15]: A woman who does all her own housework.

Shay-gitz[16]: A guy who thinks a *shikseh* is an electric razor.

Cocker: A diarrhetic diabetic.

Alta cocker: (a) An old man overdosed with milk of magnesia.
(b) One who fires blanks.

Shmonk: A rabbi who lives in a monastery.

---

[8]*extremely confused* [9]*real happiness* [10]*homosexual* [11]*gossipy woman* [12]*marriage broker* [13]*simpleton* [14]*drunk* [15]*gentile woman* [16]*gentile man*

SHMATTES

"The dress business is so bad," complained Hockman, "this last year I've been losing eight hundred dollars a week. And that's week after week after week!"

"So why don't you give up the business?"

"So how am I gonna make a living?"

*   *   *

"Is your son a good businessman?" asked Jaffe.

"My boy is so dedicated to his work," said Isaacs, "that he keeps his secretary near his bed in case he should get an idea during the night!"

*   *   *

SIGN IN WINDOW OF BANKRUPT STORE

We Undersold Everybody

41

Sol (telephoning his partner from Miami):
     How's everything in New York?
Eli: Everything's all right.
Sol: How's the weather?
Eli: How should the weather be?
Sol: How's business in the shop?
Eli: It's fine but I got bad news for you.
Sol: Whatsa matta?
Eli: We've been robbed!
Sol: Don't be silly, Eli! Put it back!

Levy closed his shop Friday night and headed for temple services, not realizing his fly was unzipped. At the entrance, he met Mrs. Weiss, the president of the Ladies' Auxiliary. "I don't like to say nothin'," she said shyly, "but your business is open!"

"You're mistaken, lady!" said Levy.

"Believe me," said Mrs. Weiss, blushing, "your business is open!"

"You're crazy!" shouted Levy, rushing inside. "I close the store every Friday to come here!"

Later, at home, Levy saw that his fly was open and realized that Mrs. Weiss had only been trying to tell him so in a delicate way. He telephoned her immediately.

"I wanna apologize!" he said, also trying to be tactful. "But tell me somethin'. When my business was open, was my salesman in or out?"

* * *

This past season in New York, business was so bad the dress manufacturers were firing their sons-in-law.

* * *

Comedy star Jackie Kahane broke up a Jewish benefit audience with this one:

Fligelman's jewelry store was held up. The owner telephoned the police, and a squad car arrived immediately.

"You wouldn't believe it!" cried Fligelman to the first cop. "I was robbed by an elephant!"

"By a *what?*" asked the policeman.

"An elephant!" exclaimed the shopkeeper. "A big truck pulled up in front of the store, an elephant got out, he gave the window a knock with his trunk, broke the glass, took all the jewelry, and left."

"An elephant from India has short ears," said the officer, "and an African elephant has long ears. What kind was it?"

"How the hell do I know?" screamed Fligelman. "He had a stocking over his head!"

*　　*　　*

TV producer Perry Cross tells this beaut to special friends:

As in most businesses, nepotism is very much part of the motion picture industry. At one time, the head of a large studio brought in the boy who had married his daughter and made him production chief.

Within six months, the young man produced three pictures that were financial disasters. The father-in-law called the boy into his office.

"It's not bad enough," he screamed, "the movies you made were lousy. And that you lost millions of dollars. But you set the son-in-law business back twenty years!"

"Jake, you took your son-in-law into the dress business with you, how's he doin'?"

"It's amazing," said Jake. "He's been with me now only two weeks and already he's a month behind in his work!"

* * *

Lubin and Weber met on Seventh Avenue. "How's business?" asked Lubin.

"Lousy!" answered Weber. "On Monday, the whole day, I sold only one suit. Tuesday, business was so bad, the salesmen were trying to sell each other. And Wednesday was even worse, yet. The man that bought the suit Monday brought it back!"

* * *

Comedian London Lee, who came from a wealthy manufacturing family, kids about it. "The nicest thing about money," says London, "is that it never clashes with anything you're wearing!"

* * *

Furriers Raskin and Miller met in Miami. "You took your son, the college boy, into the business. How's he working out?"

46

"You wouldn't believe it!" replied Miller. "He wants to cross mink with kangaroo to get fur coats with pockets in them!"

* * *

Gene McGarr, TV and motion picture director, tells about Bercovitz and Michelson, who were not only business partners but lifelong friends. They made a pact that whichever one died first, he would come back and tell the other what it was like in Heaven.

Six months later, Bercovitz died. And Michelson waited for his dear, departed friend to show some sign that he had returned to earth. Michelson passed the time impatiently hoping for and eagerly awaiting a message from Bercovitz.

Then, one year after the day of his death, Bercovitz spoke to Michelson. It was late at night. Michelson was in bed.

"Michelson! Michelson!" echoed a voice.

"Is that you, Bercovitz?"

"Yes!"

"What is it like where you are?"

"We have breakfast and then we screw. Then we eat lunch and we screw. We have dinner and then we screw!"

"Is that what Heaven is like?" asked Michelson.

"Who said anything about Heaven?" said Bercovitz. "I'm in Wisconsin and I'm a bull!"

Stan Wanderman, prez of Sunday's Child, the California dress firm, overheard this conversation at the L.A. Merchandise Mart:

"Did you hear what Melnick did with his secretary?"

"No!"

"Well, he'd been trying to make out with her for months but she kept turning him down!"

"So?"

"So, he stapled her tits together!"

"What?"

"Yeah, Melnick says his motto is: 'If you can't lick 'em—join 'em!' "

* * *

Berger and Baum were partners. While they were having lunch, Berger shouted: "Oh, my God!"

"Whatsa matta?" asked Baum.

"We went away," said Berger, "and we left the safe open!"

"Whatta you worried?" asked his partner. "We're both here!"

* * *

Irv Robbins, the brilliant guiding hand behind Baskin-Robbins, the ice cream America loves, tells about the manufacturer who phoned a friend.

"Sy, I'm in big trouble. I'm about to go bankrupt—unless I can raise some cash—and I haven't the slightest idea where I'm going to get it from."

"I'm glad to hear it," said his friend. "For a minute there I was afraid you might think you could borrow it from me!"

*   *   *

Rosenbaum sold hot dogs from a pushcart. "How's business?" asked an acquaintance.

"Could be worse!" said Rosenbaum. "I put away already two thousand dollars in the bank!"

"That's good," said the friend. "Maybe you could lend me five dollars?"

"I'm not allowed!"

"What *not allowed?*"

"I made an agreement with the bank. They agreed not to sell hot dogs if I promised I wouldn't make loans!"

*   *   *

Schecter rented space at one of those outdoor California swap meets. A woman customer picked up a broken fork and asked, "How much?"

"A penny," said Schecter.

"A penny!" grumbled the woman. "That's too much!"

"So make me an offer."

*   *   *

Krebs ran into Fink on Broadway. "Hey," cried Krebs, "I heard you had a fire!"

"Ssh!" said Fink. "It's not till next week!"

49

Sakolski got a job driving a bus. At the end of the first day he turned in the receipts—$58. The next day's returns were $61. On the third day, he brought in $56. But on the fourth day, Sakolski gave the cashier $243.

"This is great!" exclaimed the cashier. "That route never brought in that much money. What happened?"

"After three days on that lousy route," explained Sakolski, "I figured business wasn't gonna get any better, so I drove over to Broadway and worked there. Say, that street is a regular gold mine!"

* * *

Levine and Friedman, two garment workers, were strolling through Central Park one sunny spring afternoon.

"Look at them gorgeous flowers!" remarked Levine. "Are they daisies?"

"How should I know?" snapped Friedman. "I'm not in millinery!"

* * *

Joel Davis, National Media Consultants V.P., tells about Cohen and Goldberg, who were partners in the dress business. And business was terrible! A discouraged Cohen announced to his partner that he was going to change his name for good luck.

"From now on," he said, "I'm O'Brien."

That night Goldberg decided he would change his name, too. Both men instructed the switchboard operator to answer the phones: "O'Brien and O'Brien!"

Everything went fine until a caller demanded to speak to Mr. O'Brien.

"Which O'Brien do you want?" asked the operator. "Cohen or Goldberg?"

* * *

"I can't understand it," said Bloom to his partner, Rifkin. "Here we are bankrupt, through, findished—and only yesterday the President said that business was booming!"

"Maybe," said Rifkin, "the President has a better location!"

* * *

New York film producer–author Bud Greenspan remembers this classic:

Jacobs the junk peddler was trudging wearily through New York's Lower East Side one hot summer day. On his shoulder, Jacobs carried a large canvas bag loaded with iron, lead pipe, and brass that he had collected.

Jacobs, perspiring freely was making very slow progress with the heavy bag. Suddenly, a woman in a fifth-story window attracted his attention.

"Mister!" she called. "Come on up!"

Slowly, the old man climbed the four flights of stairs and finally got to the fifth floor. "Now," said the woman, "you tell little Bernard if he ain't a good boy you're gonna put him in that bag and take him away!"

51

Saul Budd of New York's Home Curtain Company contributed this doozy:

Rothstein owed a hundred dollars to Weiner. The debt was past due and Rothstein was broke, so he borrowed the hundred dollars from Spivak and paid Weiner.

A week later, Rothstein borrowed back the hundred dollars from Weiner and paid Spivak. Another week went by and Rothstein borrowed back the hundred dollars from Spivak to pay Weiner.

He repeated this transaction several times, until finally he called them up and said, "Fellas, this is a lotta bother. Why don't you two exchange the hundred dollars every week and keep me out of it!"

Mrs. Glick phoned the president of Macy's at four A.M. and said, "I just want to tell you how much I like the hat I bought!"

"That's very nice, madam!" said the executive. "But why did you have to wake me at four o'clock in the morning just to tell me that!"

"Because they just delivered it!" said Mrs. Glick.

* * *

Morty Bass, of Jeri Morton, Inc., New York's leading lingerie manufacturer, came up with this perfect solution to handling business:

In a small village in Russia, a marriage broker was trying to arrange a match between a beautiful young girl and Fishbach, a businessman. But Fishbach was stubborn. "Before I buy goods from a mill," he said, "I look at swatches. Before I get married, I gotta have a sample also."

"But my God!" exclaimed the marriage broker. "You can't ask a decent, respectable girl for a thing like that!"

"I am a businessman," said Fishbach, "and that's the way it's gonna be done!"

The broker went off sadly to talk to the girl. "I've got a fine fella for you," he began. "Lotsa money. A-one rating. But he's a little eccentric. He says he's a good businessman and he won't go into anything blind. He insists on a sample."

"Listen," said the girl, "I'm as good a businessman as he is. Samples, I wouldn't give him. But I will give him references!"

* * *

Kravitz had a heart attack. He was still a young man, but the doctors warned him not to work. "I don't know what we're gonna do," he said to his wife.

"Don't worry, sweetheart," said Mrs. Kravitz. "I can work!"

"But you've never held a job in your life! We've got thousands of dollars worth of bills."

"I could make the money as a street-walker!"

Before Kravitz could object, his wife rushed out the door. She returned that night and placed fifty dollars and ten cents on the table.

"Who the hell gave you a dime?" shrieked Kravitz.

"Everybody!" said his wife.

* * *

Steve Sheldon, Beverly Hills talent manager, tells about the two dress-firm partners:

"You bastard!" shouted Max. "You've been sleeping with my wife!"

"Honest, Max!" said his partner. "Not a wink!"

Will Marks, the New Jersey auto-body repair mogul, passed us this favorite:

Business partners Slodnick and Weinstock wanted to hire a new secretary.

"Well," said Slodnick, "you saw the three girls I just interviewed. A blonde, a brunette, and a redhead. They're all equally competent. Which one should we hire?"

"I think," announced Weinstock, "we should hire the one with the big titties!"

* * *

Stanley Ralph Ross, the celebrated Hollywood screenwriter-author and raconteur, tells about Mishkin, the dress salesman who covered the Midwest.

His first stop was Chicago. Mishkin checked into a hotel. In the middle of the night the place caught fire. Mishkin came running out on the street with nothing on—except an erection.

He stopped one of the firemen. "When you go inside," said Mishkin, "if you see a gorgeous redhead with big boobies and a nice behind, give her a screw—it's paid for already!"

* * *

In a New York City night court, three girls charged with soliciting on the street, and Liebowitz, arrested for peddling ties without a license, were brought before the judge.

"This is all a mistake, Your Honor," said the first harlot. "I was walkin' along and this guy—"

"Just a minute, young lady," said the judge. "You've been here a dozen times. One hundred dollars fine. Next!"

"I'm just a poor private secretary," said the second girl, "and I wasn't doing anything—"

"I recognize you too, miss," said the magistrate. "Two hundred dollars or ten days in jail. Next case!"

"Judge," said the third girl. "I'm a prostitute! I'm not proud of it, but it's the only way I can support my three kids. I'm guilty!"

"Young woman," said the judge, "I like your honesty. And because of it, I'm going to give you a break. Your case is dismissed. And Sergeant, give this girl fifty dollars out of the Policemen's Fund!"

Now comes poor old Liebowitz, arrested for selling ties without a license. "Your Honor," he pleaded, "I'm not gonna lie to you. I'm a prostitute!"

*　　*　　*

Comedienne Joan Rivers broke up the audience on the Johnny Carson show when she told about her high-school friend, Heidi Abramowitz.

Heidi was the school pushover. Joan met her ten years later and said, "Heidi, what are you up to?"

"Fifty dollars!" said her school chum.

Jake! I heard you had a big fire at the store!

Ssh! It's not until next weekend.

* * *

Cooperman sold strawberries off his truck out in the suburbs. He knocked on the door of a house. "Wanna buy some strawberries?"

"Come around back!" answered the pretty young blonde.

Cooperman walked to the rear, rang the bell, and the woman opened the door. To Cooperman's shock, she stood there stark naked. Not a stitch of clothes on. Cooperman started to cry.

"What's the matter?" asked the blonde.

"Today, my wife ran away with my best friend," explained Cooperman, "I lost three thousand dollars on the stock market, and now you're gonna *screw* me out of my strawberries!"

* * *

Tillie and Minnie, two old girl friends, met for lunch. "I married a wealthy clothing manufacturer," announced Tillie, "and he bought me a yacht for my birthday!"

"Astounding!" said Minnie.

"I have charge accounts in all the department stores!"

"Astounding!"

"I have a drawer full of rubies and emeralds and he bought me a twenty-five-carat diamond ring for our second anniversary!"

"Astounding!"

"What have you been doing?" asked Tillie.

"Oh," answered her friend, "going to charm school!"

"Really? What did you learn there?"

"They taught me to say 'astounding' instead of 'bullshit'!"

*   *   *

SHMOOZE

Yetta and Bessie, both grandmothers, were sitting on the sand in Miami Beach. "Isn't that ocean big?" said Yetta, gazing out at the Atlantic.

"Yeah," said Bessie, "and we're only looking at the top!"

*　*　*

Fein and Klein were sitting on a park bench. "I'll tell you the truth," said Fein, "I'm afraid to fly. Those airplanes ain't too safe!"

"Don't be a baby," said Klein, "Didn't you read last week there was a big train crash and three hundred people were killed!"

"Three hundred killed on a train—what happened?"

"An airplane fell on it!"

Smulowitz, aged eighty-three and widowed, refused to be placed in just any Miami Beach old-age home. "I won't eat anything," he declared to his son, "unless it's strictly kosher!"

The son searched for weeks and finally found a place that served meals in accordance with the Jewish dietary laws. He placed Smulowitz in the home, secure in the knowledge that his father would be eating only kosher food.

Three days later, he came for a visit and learned that the old man had left and checked into the Fontainebleau Hotel. The boy rushed over to the hotel, got a key, went upstairs, opened the door, and there was his father in bed with a blonde. They were both stark naked.

"Papa, how could you?" asked the bewildered boy.

"But look," said Smulowitz, "I'm not eating!"

Slutsky, eighty-five, was complaining to Blustein. "My housekeeper," he said, "is suing me for breach of promise!"

"At your age," inquired Blustein, "what could you promise her?"

* * *

Yetta: What's wrong with your hair, sweetheart? It looks like a wig!
Bessie: You know something, it *is* a wig!
Yetta: How do you like that—you never could tell!

* * *

Since many senior citizens have migrated to Florida, Yiddish theater has once again begun to flourish in Miami Beach. One night during a performance, the curtain suddenly came down and the stage manager stood before the audience.

"I'm sorry," he said, "but we have to stop the show. The leading man just died!"

After a gasp from the crowd, a little old lady in the balcony shouted, "Give him an enema!"

"Madam, maybe you didn't hear me! The man is dead!"

"Give him an enema!" she yelled again.

"Are you crazy or something?" retorted the stage manager. "The man is dead. An enema couldn't help him!"

"It couldn't hurt!"

Bessie: You know, before you turn around, it'll be summer again.

Yetta: So don't turn!

*　　*　　*

Grandma Weinstein was walking through the park with two little boys when she met a friend. "How old are your grandchildren?" asked the woman.

"The doctor is five and the lawyer is seven!" answered Mrs. Weinstein proudly.

*　　*　　*

Mrs. Goldstein had been a widow for some time. One day she walked into a photo shop and said to the owner, "I'd like to have this picture of my poor dead husband fixed up!"

"What is it you want done?" asked the proprietor.

"Well, this picture is the only one that I have of him, but he's wearing a hat," explained the widow. "I want you should take off the hat so I could see his gorgeous hair!"

"What kind of hair did he have?"

"Take off the hat and you'll see!" replied Mrs. Goldstein.

*　　*　　*

JEWISH GERITOL
Chicken soup spiked with Manoschewitz

Yetta: If it was summer again, where would you go on a vacation?

Bessie: Well, last year we took a trip around the world. This year we would like to go somewhere different!

* * *

Senior citizens Israel and Emma met at a singles dance on Miami Beach, and within two weeks they were married. They felt it was a perfect match, for they were both ninety years old.

On the first night of their honeymoon, they got into bed and the old man squeezed Emma's hand. She squeezed back and they fell asleep.

The second night, Israel squeezed her hand again. Emma squeezed back and they went right to sleep.

On the third night, Israel once more squeezed his bride's hand. "Not tonight," said Emma, "I've got a headache!"

* * *

"My wife and me enjoyed Japan," said Fogel to his neighbor, Goodman, reminiscing about their forty-fifth wedding anniversary trip.

"What was so terrific?" asked Goodman.

"The first night we saw a Japanese girl do her Kabuki dance," explained Fogel. "And when she danced, I could actually see her Kabuki!"

Comedian George Kirby gets howls with this one:

Mrs. Weissman had her portrait painted. When it was finished, the artist presented it to her. "How do you like it?" he asked.

"It's nice!" answered Mrs. Weissman. "But I want you should add a gold bracelet on each wrist. A pearl necklace, ruby earrings, an emerald tiara, and on each finger I want you to put a twenty-carat diamond ring!"

"But," said the bewildered artist, "why do you want to ruin a good picture with all those gaudy trinkets?"

"My husband is running around with a young chippie," explained Mrs. Weissman, "and when I die, I want her to go crazy looking for the jewelry!"

* * *

Yetta: Tell me sweetheart, what do you think of sex?
Bessie: Well, I think it's the finest department store in New York!

* * *

"Is your grandfather a religious man?" asked the young coed of her date.

"He's so Orthodox," replied the boy, "When he plays chess, he doesn't use bishops—he uses rabbis."

Lovable Jack Barry, host of TV's "The Joker's Wild," recalls an incident early in his career. He was interviewing Mr. and Mrs. Blumenthal on their sixtieth wedding anniversary.

"How old is your wife?" asked Jack.

"She's eighty-seven," said Blumenthal, "and God willing, she'll live to be a hundred!"

"And how old are you?" inquired Barry.

"I'm eighty-seven too," answered the octogenarian, "and God willing, I'll live to be a hundred and one!"

"But why," asked Jack, "would you want to live a year longer than your wife?"

"To tell you the truth," said Blumenthal, "I'd like to have at least one year of peace!"

*　　*　　*

Yetta: I've been married over forty years and I'm gettin' a little itchy. How do you start an affair?

Bessie: I don't have too much experience in that . . . but I usually start an affair with "The Star Spangled Banner."

*　　*　　*

Mrs. Markowitz was walking along the beach with her grandson when suddenly a wave came and washed the three-year-old boy out to sea.

"Oh, Lord!" cried the woman. "If you'll

just bring that boy back alive I'll do anything. I'll be the best person. I'll give to charity. I'll go to temple. Please, God! Send him back!"

At that moment, a wave washed the child back up on the sand, safe and sound. His grandmother looked at the boy and then up to the heavens.

"Okay!" she exclaimed. "So where's his hat?"

*   *   *

Bert Goldberg, prez of Texas Joyce Bertram Bath Shops chain, tells about senior citizen Berkowitz crossing Washington Avenue on Miami Beach. The elderly man was hit by a passing auto. Several passersby picked him up and laid him down on a bench.

A kindly silver-haired matron approached the injured man and said, "Are you comfortable?"

"Eh! I make a living!" sighed Berkowitz.

*   *   *

A first-time visitor to Honolulu approached the gray-haired clerk at the airport newsstand. "You look like a native," said the woman. "What is the correct way to pronounce the name of your state? Is it Hawaii or Havaii?"

"Havaii!" answered the old man.

"Thank you!"

"You're velcome!"

Four women were chatting while playing Mah-Jongg. Each took a turn bragging about her children. When three of them had finished, Mrs. Hurowitz began.

"Ladies," she said, "you don't know what it means to have a good son. My boy lives in a penthouse and he built three rooms with a kitchen especially for me. He takes me out to dinner every night. We go to the theater three times a week. Last month he took me with him on vacation to Puerto Rico. He don't do nothing without talking to me first.

"And ladies," added Mrs. Hurowitz, "my son goes to a psychiatrist five times a week. And who do you think he spends the whole time talking about? Me!"

* * *

Yetta: You know something, sweetheart? I don't like to brag, but I've been to Europe three times already.
Bessie: So what? I was *born* there!

* * *

To celebrate their thirtieth wedding anniversary, Solomon came home and presented his wife with a little monkey.

"Are you crazy or somethin'?" shouted Mrs. Solomon. "Where the hell are we gonna keep a monkey?"

"Don't worry," said Solomon, "he'll sleep right in the bed with us!"

"And what about the smell?"

"If I could stand it for thirty years—he'll get used to it also!"

*   *   *

When George Gershwin became successful he brought his immigrant father to California. One day the senior Gershwin, who spoke English with a heavy accent, was stopped by a motorcycle cop for speeding.

"You can't give me a ticket," declared Papa Gershwin. "My son is Chudge Gershwin!"

"Okay," said the cop, "I'll just give you a warning this time." As he drove away he shouted, "And give my regards to the judge!"

*   *   *

Two senior citizens in Miami were chatting. "Fishman is eighty-six," said the first man, "and he has sex relations with his wife twice a week!"

"Don't believe it!" said the second man.

"All right, ask Mrs. Fishman and her three brothers. They're always there."

"Why are her three brothers always there?"

" 'Cause Fishman fights!"

Abramson had reached the grand old age of eighty and decided to celebrate. All his life he'd been Orthodox: worn a long beard, black hat, black suit, and black overcoat.

Now, to celebrate his birthday, the octogenarian shaved off the beard. He replaced his somber black clothes with the latest-style green-checked suit, a burgundy tie, and blue striped shirt, and headed for a massage parlor. As Abramson crossed the street he was struck by a truck and killed.

In Heaven, he spoke to his Maker. "God, why me? I was a good husband! I gave to all the charities. I've always been a religious man. Why me?"

"To tell the truth," said the Lord, "I didn't *recognize* you!"

* * *

Yetta: What do you think—the truth, now—what do you think about LSD?
Bessie: I think he was a wonderful President.

* * *

Mrs. Greenfield walked into a butcher shop and said to the owner, "If you'll be so kind, I'd like you should give me a half-dozen lamb chops. How much it's gonna cost?"

"For *you*," said the butcher, "two dollars and forty cents a pound!"

"Are you crazy?" shrieked Mrs. Greenfield. "I could get across the street by Schwartz for two dollars a pound!"

"So what're you bothering me?" bellowed the butcher. "Go buy your lamb chops from Schwartz!"

"He ain't got any!"

"Listen, if I wouldn't have any," said the butcher, "I'd sell you them for a dollar forty a pound!"

*　　*　　*

Bedraggled, worried Garfinkel sat in a train holding a three-year-old boy. Every few minutes Garfinkel spanked the child.

"If you strike that baby one more time," said a woman sitting across from him, "I'll give you so much trouble you won't forget it!"

"Trouble?" said Garfinkel. "You're gonna give me trouble? Lady, my partner stole all my money and ran off with my wife and car. My daughter's in the parlor car, six months pregnant, and she ain't got no husband. My baggage is lost, I'm on the wrong train, and this little stinker just ate the tickets and threw up all over me, And lady, *you're* gonna give me trouble?"

*　　*　　*

Yetta: What d'ya think—my husband came home yesterday and told me he bought a condominium!

Bessie: That's nice! But if I was you, I would still take the pill!

When Morganstein had reached the age of sixty-five, he suddenly began chasing the young chicks. A neighbor brought his behavior to the attention of his wife. "Whatta you gonna do about it?" she asked.

"Who cares?" said Mrs. Blumenthal. "Let him chase girls! Dogs chase cars—but when they catch them, they can't drive!"

Al Jolson used to tell this one about his father. "I bought my dad an overcoat that cost a couple hundred bucks. It was beautiful! But I knew the old guy'd say two hundred dollars was too much to spend for a coat. So I told him it only cost ten dollars.

"Three weeks later, he phoned me and said, 'That overcoat was some buy for ten dollars. I sold it to your uncle Max for twenty dollars. Send me a dozen more!'"

* * *

Three grandmothers playing cards poolside at the Eden Roc in Miami Beach were joined by a fourth.

"Sit down, darling!" said the leader of the group. "We're happy you should join us. We have certain rules while we're playing. *First*, we don't talk about our children. We all got sons, doctors, lawyers . . .

"*Second*, we don't talk about our grandchildren. We all got gorgeous grandchildren.

"And *third*, we don't talk about sex! What *was*, was!"

* * *

"If we was rich," said Mrs. Aaron, "we would spend six months a year in Florida, six months in California, and six months in Europe."

"But," said Mrs. Lasky, "that makes eighteen months in one year!"

"Ain't it grand what you could do with money?"

* * *

An elderly woman climbed three flights of stairs, opened a carved mahogany door and walked into a exotically furnished reception room. A gong sounded and out of a cloud of incense appeared a beautiful brunette Oriental.

"Do you," she said softly, "wish to meet with His Omnipotence, the wise, all-knowing, all-seeing guru, Maharishi Naru?"

"Yeah," said the gray-haired woman. "Tell Sheldon his mother is here from the Bronx!"

* * *

"Lieberman must be well on in age!"

"Yes, poor man! He's so old he gets winded playing checkers!"

* * *

Yetta: What would you do if you found a million dollars?

Bessie: Well, if it was a *poor person* that lost it, I'd give it back!

For centuries, European Jews were the victims of organized persecution, called pogroms. These pogroms took place so often that Jews developed a sense of humor about them.

In a small town in Poland, soldiers broke into the house of Ostrovsky and his family. Living with him were his wife, three daughters, two sons, and his aged mother.

"Line up!" shouted the sergeant in charge. "We're gonna beat up all the men and rape all the women!"

"Wait!" pleaded Ostrovsky. "You can wallop me and my sons, abuse my wife and daughters, but please sir, I beg you . . . don't rape my mother! She's seventy-five years old!"

"Shut up!" yelled the old woman. "A pogrom is a pogrom!"

Mrs. Goldfarb walked into a kosher butcher shop, asked the owner for a "fresh chicken," and immediately began inspecting it. She lifted the wing, stuck her nose underneath, and declared, "Phew! It smells!"

Then she pulled up a leg, sniffed and said, "Feh!"

After smelling the hind end, Mrs. Goldfarb held her nose and exclaimed, "It stinks! You call this a fresh chicken!"

"Tell me, lady," said the butcher, "you could stand such an inspection?"

* * *

Bernstein, anxious for a relaxing steam bath at the Turkish baths, could not get in because it was ladies' night. Undaunted, he went to a costume shop, rented a dress and wig, and entered the baths.

Draped in a sheet, Bernstein headed for the steam room. However, unbeknownst to him, the lower half of his sheet caught on a nail, exposing his body from the waist down.

A sweet, white-haired, woman stopped him and said, "I beg your pardon, madam! But your baby's leg is sticking out!"

* * *

Feingold, on his deathbed, was surrounded by his children. "Don't worry, Papa, we'll have a big funeral," declared his eldest son. "There'll be a hundred limousines, ten cars with flowers—"

"We don't need all that!" interrupted Feingold's second son. "Fifty limos and five cars with flowers is more than enough!"

"Whatta ya makin' such a big deal?" said the dying man's youngest son. "We don't need any flowers. We'll just have the immediate family! Two cars is enough!"

At that moment, Feingold raised himself up and said, "Listen, boys! Just hand me my pants and I'll *walk* to the cemetery!"

* * *

Two partners, Abrams and Schneider, agreed that whoever died first, the other one was to put five thousand dollars in the coffin. Abrams died, and Schneider fulfilled his part of the contract. He put in a check.

* * *

Meyer: I heard your father passed away.
Israel: Yeah, he died and left me four thousand dollars to buy a stone to remember him by.
Meyer: Isn't that a new diamond ring you're wearing?
Israel: Yeah, that's the stone I bought to remember him by.

Yetta: Well, goodbye, sweetheart! If I
live, I'll see you Wednesday!
Bessie: Okay.
Yetta: If not, Thursday!

*   *   *

Actor-comedian Jesse White tells about
the apartment house in the Bronx occupied
entirely by Jewish tenants. McMurphy was
the janitor.

"How do you like working here?" asked
Wasserman, one of the building's occupants.

"Oh, I love working for the Jews!" said
McMurphy. "In fact, I'll tell you a little
secret. I've made love to every woman in
this building—except one!"

Wasserman rushed upstairs. "You know
what the janitor just told me," he exclaimed to Mrs. Wasserman. "He's made
love to every woman in this building except one!"

"Well," said his wife, "it must be that
stuck-up Mrs. Rudnick on the second
floor!"

*   *   *

SHTOOPS

Flinging epithets at one's enemies is a time-honored device to vent anger and frustration. But Jews throughout the centuries developed the knack of framing contemptuous word pictures into a fine art.

As with all phrases taken from another language, these expletives lose something in the translation from their original Yiddish. Nevertheless, here are some classic Jewish curses:

You should only starve for a piece of bread and come to me for help and I should be too poor to help you!

* * *

All your teeth should fall out except one and that should have a toothache.

* * *

There should grow in your stomach a trolley car and I should be the conductor going, "Clang! Clang! Clang!"

You should live the rest of your life like a chandelier! You should hang all day and burn all night.

May you become a widower before your wife's death.

If you don't live to be an old maid, may you live to be a young widow.

May your wife be a witch who takes after her mother, and may you all live together in a one-room house.

You should grow like an onion, with your head in the ground and you feet in the air.

May the fleas from a thousand camels infest your armpits.

You should inherit a big house that has a thousand rooms and each room should have a featherbed and you should have a fever of 105 that should toss you from one bed to another and another and another!

Beets should only grow from your stomach and you should only pee borscht.

The fountain pen you gave me for Chanukah—it should only run from your nose like it leaks in my pocket.

You should have ten penthouses in ten Park Avenue buildings and in each one you should have a gorgeous blonde waiting to do your every wish and in front of each of these ten buildings you should have a Rolls Royce with a chauffeur and every morning you should get into each car and your chauffeur should drive you to a different doctor and not one doctor should know what's wrong with you!

* * *

SHOCHETS

What word beginning with "A" means "prince" in Jewish?
A doctor!

* * *

A psychiatrist and a proctologist became good friends and agreed to share offices to cut down on expenses. To economize even further, they had just one sign printed:
Dr. Marvin Hornstein, *Psychiatrist*
Dr. David Slodnick, *Proctologist*
SPECIALIZING IN ODDS AND ENDS

* * *

Dr. Arnold Epstein, Beverly Hills heart surgeon, gave this advice to a complaining hospital intern: "You can become a millionaire and immortal at the same time. All you have to do is invent a cure for which there is no disease."

After taking off her clothes for an examination, Mrs. Greenberg sat on the table. "Lady," said the doctor, "I have to tell you that you are by far the dirtiest, filthiest, most unclean woman I have ever examined in my life!"

"How d'ya like that!" said Mrs. Greenberg. "The doctor I went to yesterday said the same thing!"

"Then why did you come here?"

"I wanted to get another opinion!" answered Mrs. Greenberg.

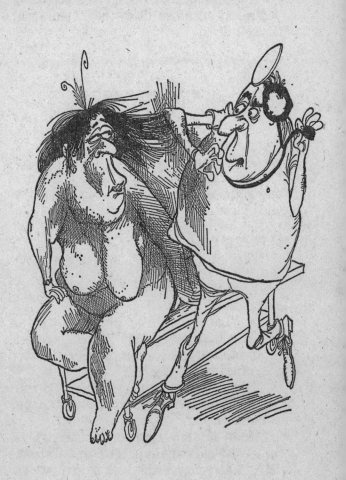

"Your cousin's a famous surgeon?"

"A genius! He's the kind of a doctor, if you're at death's door—he'll pull you through!"

* * *

JEWISH PENICILLIN
Chicken soup

* * *

After her examination, Mrs. Kurtz removed three one-dollar bills from her purse and placed them on the doctor's desk.

"That's only three dollars," said the M.D. "My fee is ten!"

"They told me five!" said the woman sweetly.

* * *

CONSULTATION
A medical term meaning "share the wealth"

* * *

Doctor Kaplan approached his eighty-three-year-old patient in the hospital room. "Mr. Adler, you're the best patient we've ever had in this hospital, and because you've been so cooperative I'm going to tell you something we don't usually tell a patient. I'm sorry—but you're going to die. Is there anyone you'd like to see?"

"Yes," answered Adler. "I'd like to see another doctor!"

* * *

Stein, aged sixty-five, visited the office of his son, Dr. Stein, and asked for something that would increase his sexual potency. The M.D. gave his father a shot and then refused to accept a fee. Nevertheless, Stein insisted on giving him ten dollars.

A week later, Stein was back for another injection, and this time handed his son twenty dollars.

"But Pop! Shots are only ten dollars!"

"Take it!" said Stein. "The extra ten is from Mama!"

* * *

On his seventy-fifth birthday, Turtletaub rushed into a physician's office. "Doctor," he exclaimed, "I've got a date tonight with a twenty-two-year-old girl . . . you gotta give me something to pep me up!"

The M.D. smiled sympathetically and supplied the old man with a prescription. Later that night, out of curiosity, the medical man phoned his elderly patient. "Did the medicine help?"

"It's wonderful!" replied Turtletaub. "Seven times already!"

"That's great!" agreed the doctor. "And what about the girl?"

"The girl?" said Turtletaub. "She didn't get here yet!"

"Is your nephew Irving a good doctor?"

"Good? He's such a lovely boy, last year I needed an operation and I couldn't afford it. So he touched up the X-rays!"

* * *

"My son-in-law, the doctor, has been treating a patient for yellow jaundice for twenty years! He just found out the man was Chinese."

"Ain't that somethin'?"

"What's terrible is—he cured him!"

* * *

After examining Bloomberg, the doctor said, "You're going to need quite a bit of treatment. The fee will be a hundred dollars."

"Doctor, I'm a poor man," pleaded Bloomberg. "Give me a break!"

"All right," said the physician, "make it fifty dollars."

"Times are bad, Doctor, and I have three children to support!"

"Okay—twenty-five dollars!"

"I only work three days a week—couldn't you make it a little less?"

"Make it ten dollars!" said the frustrated physician. "But why do you come to me? I'm a specialist. You know I'm expensive!"

"When it comes to my health," said Bloomberg, "money is no object!"

Sid Berk, California's Vogue Shoes prez, broke up pals at the health club with this one:

A man sat before Dr. Gluckstein, the aged but renowned urinary-disorders specialist.

"My trouble," complained the man, "is that I can't pee!"

"How old are you?" asked Dr. Gluckstein.

"I'm ninety-three!"

"It's all right," said the famous urologist. "You peed enough!"

* * *

"Doctor, my feet hurt so bad—when I leave here, what should I do?"

"Take a taxi!" advised the podiatrist.

* * *

PSYCHIATRIST
A Jewish doctor who hates the sight of blood

* * *

"I got good news and bad news about our son." said Mrs. Smuckler to her husband.

"Give me the bad news first!" said Mr. Smuckler.

"Our boy's become a homosexual!"

"And what's the good news?"

"He's going with a rich doctor!"

Feldman, seated at the same table in a restaurant with Lerner, noticed that the poor man had nothing but gums to chew with. Feldman pulled some false teeth out of his pocket and offered them to his dinner companion. They were too loose.

Feldman volunteered another set of dentures. This time they were too tight. The next set, however, fit perfectly.

"Thanks very much!" said Lerner. "What a pleasure to sit at the same table with such a fine dentist!"

"Whatta ya talkin', dentist!" said Feldman. "I'm an *undertaker!*"

* * *

Steinberg felt a cold coming on, so he went to a doctor. Before Steinberg could explain his ailment, the nurse sent him into the next room and told him to strip. A man was standing there with his clothes under one arm and a package under the other.

"Can you imagine," complained Steinberg to his companion, "that nurse sent me in here to take off all my clothes—I only got a sore throat!"

"That's nothing!" said the man. "I came here to deliver a package!"

* * *

Doctor: All right, what seems to be the trouble?

Pincus: You went to school for ten years
... you tell me!

*   *   *

"Mrs. Sussman," said the psychiatrist, "there's nothing physically wrong with your little boy. But I'm afraid he does have an Oedipus complex!"

"Oedipus, shmedipus!" retorted Mrs. Sussman. "Just so long as he loves his mother!"

*   *   *

LOX
A herring with high blood pressure

*   *   *

Mrs. Garfunkel needed an intimate examination and decided that instead of going to a regular doctor she would patronize her son's friend, a gynecologist. Besides, since the boy had grown up in the neighborhood, she felt more comfortable about him.

Once Mrs. Garfunkel was on the examination table, the doctor, wearing rubber gloves, inspected and probed the woman's most private parts.

When he finished, Mrs. Garfunkel said, "Sammy, your mama knows you're making a living like this?"

Vaudevillians Smith and Dale were famous for their doctor sketch. This is a tiny chunk:

Dale: What are your fees, Doctor?

Smith: I charge ten dollars the first visit and five dollars for the second visit.

Dale: Well, Doctor, it's nice to see you again! What should I do?

Smith: Take the same medicine I gave you last time!

* * *

Mrs. Weinberg, age eighty-six, walked into a doctor's office to be examined.

"What's your complaint?" asked the M.D.

"I feel tired and run-down!" she said.

"I'm sorry," said the physician, "but I can't make you any younger!"

"All I want you should do," said Mrs. Weinberg, "is make me older!"

* * *

"Stop shaking your arms and making those pained faces at me," said Dr. Braverman, the dentist. "I haven't even started drilling yet!"

"I know that!" exclaimed Mrs. Kutcher, pulling the cotton out of her mouth to speak. "But you're standing on my corns!"

Doctor: The check you gave me came back!

Krinsky: So did my arthritis.

* * *

Comedian Buddy Lester heard a fellow seeking advice from a doctor at a cocktail party. "Hey, Doc," asked the man, "how do you stop a Jewish girl from screwing?"

"Marry her!"

* * *

Overheard at the same cocktail party:

"Morris, I want you to meet Doctor Sussman! Don't stand up, he's only a dentist!"

* * *

Dr. Vogel, the dentist, finished his examination on a pretty young patient. "Miss Bassman," he said, "I'm afraid I'm going to have to pull out your wisdom teeth!"

"Oh, my!" exclaimed the girl. "I'd rather have a baby!"

"Well," said Dr. Vogel, "could you make up your mind so I can adjust the chair?"

Dr. Ramon Spritzler, Beverly Hills internist, relaxes patients with this beaut:

Klein, eighty-seven, married a twenty-one-year-old girl. After their honeymoon, he went to a doctor. "She's only a young girl," said Klein. "I want to keep her satisfied. What should I do?"

"My advice," said the physician, "is that you should take in a boarder!"

One year later, Klein revisited the medical man. "How's your wife?" asked the doctor.

"She's pregnant!" said the old man proudly.

"And how's the boarder?"

"She's pregnant, too!"

*　　*　　*

SHABBES

"Rabbi Jacobs, I need fifty dollars to get out of debt," sobbed Gottlieb. "I keep praying to God for help but He doesn't send it!"

"Don't lose faith," said the rabbi. "Keep praying."

After Gottlieb left his house, the rabbi felt sorry for him. "I don't make much money," he thought, "but that poor man needs it. I'll give him twenty-five dollars out of my own pocket."

A week later, the rabbi stopped Gottlieb and said, "Here, God sent this to you!"

Back in his home, Gottlieb bowed his head. "Thank you, Lord!" he said. "But next time you send money, don't send it through Rabbi Jacobs—that crook kept half of it!"

Siegel and Posner, complete strangers, were sitting across from each other, nude, in the steam room. "I never met you before," said Siegel, "and yet I'll bet you were born in Brooklyn!"

"That's right!" said Posner.

"In fact," said Siegel to his naked companion, "you're from my old neighborhood, Bensonhurst, and you went to the Seventy-ninth Street Synagogue, and your rabbi was Nathan Nussbaum!"

"Amazing!" said Posner. "You can tell all that just by looking at me?"

"Of course," said Siegel. "Rabbi Nussbaum always did cut on the bias!"

* * *

"I'm so upset," said Hershberg to a rabbi. "I took my son-in-law into my clothing business and yesterday I caught him kissing one of the models!"

"Have a little patience!" advised the rabbi. "After all, guys will be guys. So he kissed one of the models, it's not so terrible."

"But you don't understand," said Hershberg. "I make *men's* clothes!"

* * *

The sexton ran into the rabbi's office and exclaimed excitedly, "Rabbi, I have terrible news to report! Burglars must've broken in last night—they stole ninety thousand dollars' worth of pledges!"

* * *

Two rabbis were having lunch. "Some of my congregation is switching over to the Quakers!" complained the first.

"Is that a fact?" said the second.

"Yes, some of my best Jews are Friends!"

* * *

Scientists concluded that the icecap was going to melt and the whole world would be flooded within six months. When the news broke, religious leaders went into deep conference.

The Protestant hierarchy released a statement: "Because of the impending disaster Protestants will go to church and pray for two hours every day."

Then the Catholics made an announcement: "Because of the coming deluge, Catholics will make every other day—all day—a day of prayer for the next six months!"

Rabbis from all over the land convened, then they too issued a message to the world: "Because the whole world will be flooded in six months, Jews will learn how to live underwater!"

I heard Alan King tell this gem:

A little boy came home from Sunday School, and his father said, "What did the rabbi teach you today?"

"Well," said the youngster, "two thousand years ago the Jews wanted to escape from the bad Egyptians, so Moses had the Jews build this suspension bridge across the Red Sea. Then they loaded it down with dynamite. The Jews escaped across the bridge, and when all the Egyptians chased them, they blew up the bridge and all the Egyptians were drowned."

"Is that what the rabbi told you?" asked the surprised father.

"No," said the boy, "but you'd never believe the crazy story he *did* tell us!"

"How come you decided to become a Jew?"

"Well, I used to be an atheist, but I gave it up!"

"Why?"

"No holidays!"

* * *

Everything in Southern California is a little far out—even religion. There's a Reform temple in Beverly Hills that's so Reform that on the holiest of days—Yom Kippur—they have a sign on the door saying "Closed for the Jewish Holidays."

* * *

Samuels met Bloomfeld at the race track. "How is it," asked Samuels, "you win all the time and I always lose?"

"Because," boasted Bloomfeld, "before I come to the track on Saturday afternoon I go to the temple and I pray."

Samuels decided to follow his friend's example. The following Saturday they met again, but Samuels was still a loser. "I don't understand it," he complained. "I went to the temple this morning and I lost every race!"

"What temple did you go to?" asked Bloomfeld.

"Beth Israel!"

"You idiot!" cried Bloomfeld. "That's for trotters!"

* * *

Monty Hall, America's beloved TV host of "Let's Make a Deal," is also one of Hollywood's biggest fund-raisers. Here is a story he tells at charity dinners:

Shimkin had been shipwrecked for twenty years on a desert island when finally he was rescued by a passing ship.

"What did you do to keep busy all those years?" asked the captain of the rescue vessel.

"I went into the building business!" replied Shimkin. Whereupon he took the captain to a corner of the island and showed him a beautiful synagogue.

"That's incredible!" said the sailing master.

"That's nothin'," said Shimkin. This time he led him to the opposite end of the island and displayed another magnificently constructed house of worship.

"I don't understand," said the captain. "You're the only person on the island— why did you need two synagogues?"

"This one I belong to," explained Shimkin, "but the other one—I wouldn't set foot inside if they paid me!"

Some Jewish boys don't have the same attitude toward religion as their fathers. Eisenstein sent a telegram to his son: DON'T FORGET YOM KIPPUR STARTS TOMORROW.

The boy sent a wire back: PUT $100 ON THE NOSE FOR ME.

*   *   *

Schlossberg was a very religious man. While visiting a cousin in St. Louis, he said to him, "Our rabbi is so holy that he talks to God."

"Talks with God?" said his relative. "How do you know that?"

"He told us so himself!" replied Schlossberg.

"But maybe he lied!"

"Dumbbell! Would a man who talks to God tell lies?"

*   *   *

The rabbi had stood before the synagogue's board of directors for almost an hour pleading with them to buy a chandelier for the temple.

When he'd finished, Blum, the elderly president, stood up. "What're we wasting time talkin'?" he demanded. "First of all, a chandelier—we ain't got nobody could even *spell* it!

"Second, we ain't got nobody here who could *play* it!

"And third, what we need in the synagogue is more *light!*"

* * *

Jacobson, aged ninety, had lived through beatings in Polish pogroms, concentration camps in Germany, and dozens of other anti-Semitic experiences.

"Oh, Lord!" he prayed, sitting in synagogue. "Isn't it true that we are your chosen people?"

And from the heavens boomed a voice: "Yes, Jacobson, the Jews are my chosen people!"

"Well, then," wailed the old man, "isn't it time you chose somebody else?"

* * *

Rabbi Birnbaum sat in temple all alone, tears streaming down his cheeks. He just learned that his only son had deserted the faith of his forefathers and had become a Protestant.

The rabbi was sobbing uncontrollably when suddenly he heard the voice of God: "What is troubling you?"

"I'm so ashamed," cried the Rabbi. "My only son gave up being a Jew and became a Christian!"

"*Yours* too?" replied the Lord.

Monahan stopped his friend Weinberg and said, "Say, I've always been meanin' to ask you a question!"

"You could ask me anything!" said Weinberg.

"What is a *bris*?"

"My friend," said Weinberg, "you know the expression 'you can't take it with you'?"

"Yeah!"

"A *bris* means you can't even keep it all while you're here!"

* * *

Ben Hakim, the Honolulu huckster of precious gems, tells about Rabbi Resnick and Father Foley, seated next to each other on a jet to Chicago. "Say, Father," said the rabbi, "have you ever been out with a woman?"

"Of course not!" exclaimed the shocked priest. "That would be like your eating ham!"

"I'll tell you something," said the rabbi. "I've tried both and believe me, there's no comparison!"

* * *

Kramer and Grosberg were Orthodox and even wore beards, black hats, and long black coats. They passed a Catholic church, peeked inside, and noticed a service in progress. Friends and relatives had crowded together in the pews to witness a group of nuns taking their vows.

"Those girls," explained Kramer, "are becoming the brides of Christ!"

"Let's go in and take a look!" said Grosberg.

The moment they sat down to watch the marriage ceremony, an usher walked up to them. "What are you two doing here?"

"It's all right," said Kramer. "We're from the groom's side!"

*　　*　　*

Father Duffy and Rabbi Muchnik were chatting at a town meeting. "Could I ask you a question?" inquired Father Duffy.

"Of course," said Rabbi Muchnik.

"It's always been my understanding that the Apostles were Jews. Isn't that correct?"

"Absolutely right!" replied the rabbi.

"Then how the deuce did the Jews let go of a good thing like the Catholic Church and let the Eye-talians grab it?"

*　　*　　*

Father Clanahan and Father McNurty were concluding a theological discussion. As they parted, Father Clanahan said, "By the way, what are you giving up for Lent?"

"Matzoh-ball soup!" replied the other priest.

McLain dialed the number of a large law firm. When the switchboard operator answered, he asked, "Is Mr. Berkowitz in?"

"No, he's not," she said. "This is Yom Kippur."

"Well," said McLain, "when do you expect him, Miss Kippur?"

* * *

Father Shannon and Rabbi Rudnick were sitting ringside at the prizefights. Just before the main event, one of the fighters knelt in his corner and crossed himself.

"Tell me," said the rabbi, "does that help?"

"Not a bit if he can't fight!" answered the priest.

* * *

Shulman had been given the job of repainting the town's Catholic church. After a week, the Mother Superior called him into her office.

"Mr. Shulman, we're very pleased with your work," she said, "but there are some things you must stop doing if you are to continue here!"

"Yes?" said Shulman.

"First," said the Mother Superior, "remove your hat when you come into the church. Second, don't wash your hands in the holy water. And third, stop calling me Mother *Shapiro!*"

* * *

Young Sammy was playing with little Timothy in the street. Suddenly, Timothy exclaimed: "My priest knows more than your rabbi!"

"Why shouldn't he?" said Sammy. "You tell him everything!"

* * *

Robert Briscoe, the Jewish former lord mayor of Dublin, had the typical Irish charm and wit. He once said that after he was elected, out of deference to him, they called leprechauns "lepre*cohens*."

At a fund-raising affair in New York, Briscoe told the audience that most of the four thousand Jews in Ireland were Orthodox. Recently, however, a Reform synagogue had been built in Dublin.

"As you know," he said, "Ireland's population is ninety-five percent Catholic, and foreigners on sightseeing trips often ask what the new building is. Cabdrivers have been known to answer, 'Oh, that's the new Protestant synagogue!'"

Sam Young, West Coast Manager of *Amusement Business Magazine*, made this contribution:

Rabbi Grossman and Father O'Malley were seated beside each other at a banquet. "Have some ham," offered the priest.

"I'm afraid not," answered the rabbi.

"C'mon, try some," the priest encouraged. "It's real good!"

"Thanks, but I don't eat that kind of meat because of my religion."

"It's really delicious!" said Father O'Malley five minutes later. "You oughta try this ham, you'd like it!"

"No thank you!" replied Rabbi Grossman.

After dinner, the two men shook hands. "Tell me," said the Jewish clergyman, "do you enjoy sex with your wife?"

"Oh, Rabbi, you should know I'm not allowed to be married," said the priest. "I can't have sex!"

"You ought to try it," said the rabbi. "It's better than ham!"

* * *

Abie wanted to marry his Irish Rose, and they stood in the temple office. "I'd be very happy to officiate," said the rabbi, "but I'd like to be assured that Rose has a little Jew in her!"

"Oh, I do!" the bride-to-be exclaimed. "Abie couldn't wait!"

The Jews and the Irish have traditionally stood side by side in the bonds of good fellowship. So much so, that should there ever be a Jewish-Catholic prayer, it would begin:

"Oy vay, Maria!"

*　　*　　*

THE CHILDREN OF ISRAEL

A Christian visiting the Holy Land struck up a conversation with a Palestinian.

"I'm really surprised that you and the Arabs can't get together peacefully."

"My dear man," said the Israeli, "the Jews are a very argumentative people. The only thing you can get two Jews to agree upon is what a third Jew should give to charity."

* * *

The voice of the stewardess on the Israeli charter airliner came over the loudspeaker: "Welcome on board. Your hostesses are Mrs. Dora Fein and Mrs. Fay Hershberg and, of course, my son, the pilot."

Two Christians, Walters and Smythe, met on a pilgrimage to Palestine during Holy Week.

"It's a shame all those differences between the Arabs and the Israelis," said Walters.

"Yes," agreed Smythe, "They ought to settle their problems in a true Christian spirit."

*   *   *

Every year, dignitaries of the Church come from Rome to Israel and a time-honored ceremony is reenacted. One of the chief rabbis hands a jewel-covered scroll to a visiting priest who holds the scroll for a minute, shakes his head, and then returns it to the rabbi until the next year.

This year, however, the rabbi and the priest involved in the ceremony grew curious about the scroll and decided to open it. They removed the jeweled covering, then unrolled yards and yards of yellowed parchment with long columns of numbers on it and some blurred words. The rabbi put on his glasses and finally managed to read the ancient Hebrew letters. It was the bill for the Last Supper.

Kay Rappeport, the jolly Little Rock, Arkansas, KLAZ radio producer, sent along this jovial joke:

Why did the Jews win the Middle East War in 6 days?

Because the equipment was rented!

* * *

New Yorker Friedman joined the Israeli Army. After a week he asked for a 3-day leave of absence.

"What are you, nuts?" the Colonel asked. "You're in the army a week and already you want a pass? To get a 3-day pass you have to do something sensational."

The next day Friedman came back to camp driving an Arab tank. "How did you do it?" asked the amazed Colonel.

"I took one of our tanks and drove toward Jordan," said Friedman. "I saw one of their tanks coming toward me. The Arab put up a white flag, and I put up a white flag. I said to him, 'Do you want to get a 3-day pass?' He said, 'Yes,' so we exchanged tanks."

Miriam Udell, the bouncy Brooklyn homemaker, tells about Fishbeck and Bloomberg who migrated to Israel and became bounty hunters. They were offered $25 for each Arab they captured.

On their first night out they went to sleep on the Left Bank. The next morning Fishbeck woke up and discovered they were surrounded by 10,000 Arabs.

"Wake up," cried Fishbeck, "Wake up! We're rich!"

*　　*　　*

"Wake up, wake up! We're rich!"

ISRAELI NAVY SLOGAN

Don't Give Up the Ship—Sell It

* * *

Mintz, a former New York dress manufacturer, joined the Israeli Navy on maneuvers in the Mediterranean. Mintz was the lookout on deck of a submarine, the captain down below. Peering through his binoculars, Mintz suddenly froze in fear. He grabbed the speaking tube and shouted, "Captain, on the horizon, a destroyer, it's Egyptian. Fire a torpedo!"

"Okay, Mintz, I'll keep watch on my radar."

A few minutes later. "Captain, two hundred yards away, the enemy. Fire a torpedo!"

"Okay, Mintz, I have him sighted on my radar. I know when to act. Relax."

"Captain, a hundred yards away, a boat, Egyptian. Fire a torpedo!"

"Relax, Mintz, I know when."

"Captain, fifty yards away, an Egyptian boat! Fire a torpedo! I'll pay for it!"

Pushkin and Karpinsky, two refugees, were working on the Negev. They were tired and weary trying to make the desert bloom. "Who needs it?" said Pushkin. "So we were persecuted a little in Russia, but who worked so hard?"

"You jerk," said Karpinsky, "don't you realize that Moses walked 40 years, day and night, just to get here? This is the Promised Land."

"Listen," said Pushkin, "if Moses had walked a few more days we'd be on the Riviera right now."

*　　*　　*

Eisenstein, aged and bearded, stood in a crowded bus that was making its way through traffic from Jaffa to Tel Aviv.

A 10-year-old boy, unable to reach the straps to balance himself, was hanging on to the man's beard for support.

After awhile the old man couldn't take it any longer. "Say, boy," asked Eisenstein, "would you mind letting go of my beard?"

"What's the matter?" answered the youngster, "are you getting off here?"

Jacobs and Lipkin, two Israeli commandos, were about to be shot by the Arabs.

Jacobs said, "I think I'm gonna ask for a blindfold."

Lipkin said, "Jake, don't make trouble."

* * *

A small vessel was sailing in Israeli water when a Jewish boat pulled alongside. A man on the deck of the sailboat yells, "Ahoy."

A sailor on the Israeli boat shouted back, "Ahoy, yoi, yoi!"

* * *

An Israeli bomber pilot radioed his base commander, "I'm flying over a brand new steel mill built for the Egyptians by the Russians on the Upper Nile and I've got 3 bombs left. Shall I blow up the mill?"

"Don't be a dumbbell!" answered the commander. "Leave that mill alone. Mismanaging it will cost the Arabs at least $10 million a year!"

Kornblum, aged 76, took an unscheduled flight in the Middle East and suddenly found that two big Arabs had also boarded the airplane. One of them said, "Hey, Jew, we want the window seat!" So he gave it to them.

The plane took off and one of the Arabs said, "Go to the back of the plane and get me some coffee!" Kornblum got the coffee and when he came back the other Arab said, "Now *I* want coffee!"

The old man rushed back and got him some, but by the time he got back the fellow's companion wanted a refill. The two kept him running back and forth for an hour. Finally, Kornblum flopped down in a seat, exhausted. One of the Arabs said, "Jew, what do you think of the world?"

"Well, it's in terrible shape," said Kornblum. "In India, Mohammedans are killing Muslims. In Ireland, Protestants are killing Catholics. And in airplanes Jews are pissing in Arabs' coffee!"

*   *   *

How do they take the census in Israel? They roll a nickel down the street.

Berkowitz, a salesman, while driving through the Negev desert, saw an Arab lying on the sand. Berkowitz rushed to the man's side and lifted him up. The Arab whispered, "Water, Effendi, Water!"

"This is Kismet," exclaimed Berkowitz. "Are you in luck. I happen to have in my suitcase the finest selection of ties you ever saw."

"No," wailed the Arab, "Water! Water!"

"These ties you could see right now in the King David Hotel—$15 a piece, for *you* only $10!"

"Please, Effendi, I need water!"

"Look, you seem like a nice person. I'm known all over the Negev as 'Honest Abe.' Whatever kind of ties you like—silk, wool, rep, crepe—you can have what you want . . . $8 each!"

"I need w-w-water!"

(*con't*)

"*I need water!*"

"All right, you drive a hard bargain. Tell you what—take your pick. Two for $10."

"Pul—eeze, give me water!"

"Oh, you want water?" said Berkowitz. "Why didn't you say so? All you gotta do is crawl 500 feet to that sand dune, hang a right for a quarter of a mile, you'll come to Poopy's Pyramid Club. He'll give you all the water you want!"

The Arab slowly crawled to the sand dune, turned right and with his last remaining strength came to the door of the club. Poopy, the owner, was standing out front. "Water! Water!" begged the Arab.

"You want water? You came to the right place! I got well water, seltzer water, whatever water you want, I got on the inside. The only thing is—you can't go in without a tie."

"You can't go in . . ."

The Israelis are very critical of their government leaders. One former prime minister, who has since died, was always being berated for his inability to make a decision.

As a resident of Jerusalem once said, "When he goes to a restaurant and the waiter asks, 'Tea or coffee?' he always answers, 'Half and half!'"

* * *

Private Goldman stood guard on one side of a hill.

On the opposite side was an Arab guard.

Goldman kept shouting, "Thirteen! Thirteen! Thirteen!"

The annoyed Arab guard called over, "What are you screaming out 'Thirteen' all the time for? What does that mean?"

"Come over here," said Goldman, "I'll show you."

The Arab guard climbed up and the Israeli said, "Look over that side."

Goldman kicked the Arab over the top and began hollering, "Fourteen! Fourteen! Fourteen!"

Fogel, a native of Haifa, passed away and went below. He was amazed to discover lush vegetation, rambling brooks, and pretty little lakes that surrounded him everywhere.

"You look surprised," said an Arab resident of the place.

"I expected Hell to be hot and dry and arid," said the Israeli, "but here are fruit trees, vegetables, flowers, and green grass. You call this Hell?"

"Well, it used to be hot and barren," explained the Arab. "But then those Israelis started coming down here and they irrigated the hell out of the place!"

* * *

Outside a Dublin pub a man put a gun to McQuillan's head and demanded an answer, "Are you a Catholic or a Protestant?"

Oh, God, thought the poor Irishman, *if I say Catholic I might get it. If I say Protestant he'll kill me.* He turned to the man who threatened him and said, "Well, O'im an Arab!"

"Oh, my," exclaimed the man, "ain't I the luckiest Israeli in Ireland."

HEARD ON ISRAELI RADIO:

"This is Station KVY, Tel Aviv, 1400 on your dial, but for you 1395!"

* * *

Morty Bass, the laughing lingerie mogul, entertains buyers with this magnificent bit of merriment:

Old Mrs. Abramson stood at the Wailing Wall hysterically crying and pounding the bricks. A tourist walked over to her and said, "Madam, there's no need for you to cry. The Jews now have a homeland, a place to go to. After 2000 years you finally have the country you've always wanted. Good heavens, why are you crying?"

The old lady said, "I want to go to Miami Beach!"

* * *

At Lockheed a part was needed for a new airplane, and an announcement was sent around the world in order to get the lowest bid. From Poland came a bid of $3000. England offered to build the part for $6000. The asking price from Israel was $9000.

Richardson, the engineer in charge of constructing the new plane, decided to visit each country to find the reason behind the disparity of the bids. In Poland, the manufacturer explained, "$1000 for the materials needed, $1000 for the labor, and $1000 for overhead and a tiny profit."

In England, Richardson inspected the part and found that it was almost as good as the Polish-made one. "Why are you asking $6000?" inquired the engineer.

"$2000 for material," explained the Englishman, "$2000 for labor and $2000 for our expenses and a small profit."

In Israel, the Lockheed representative wandered through a back alley, into a small shop and encountered an elderly man who had submitted the bid of $9000. "Why are you charging that much?" he asked.

"Well," said the old Jew, "$3000 for you, $3000 for me and $3000 for the schlemiel in Poland."

The Israeli Army ordered some surplus tanks from the Italians. Major Rosenberg, the officer making the purchase, noticed there were 2 different models, one $50 less than the other.

"Why two models?" he asked Russo, the Italian in charge.

"For the extra $50," replied Russo, "you get back-up lights."

"Give us the less expensive brand," said the Israeli, "and sell the others to the Egyptians!"

*　　*　　*

BUSINESS IS BUSINESS

Two cloak and suit manufacturers, Ornstein and Raskin, were sitting in their empty offices wailing over the sudden drop in business. "I wish Gabriel would blow his horn," said Ornstein.

"Why?" asked Raskin.

"All the dead people'll come to life," explained Ornstein, "and they'll all need clothes."

* * *

Resnick and Schechter, two garment men, were sitting in a restaurant during the slack season.

"Did you hear about Sidney?" asked Resnick. "His place burned down."

"Yeah?" said Schechter. "He's a nice fellow. He deserves it."

During the French Revolution, when the guillotine was being used almost around the clock, Slutsky lived in a small village outside of Paris. One morning he met Flambeau, who had just returned from the city.

"What's happening there in Paris?" asked Slutsky.

"Conditions are absolutely horrible," replied the Frenchman. "They're cutting off heads by the thousands."

"*Oy*," moaned Slutsky "and me in the hat business!"

*   *   *

One bright school morning the teacher turned to her class and asked, "All those pupils who want to go to Heaven, raise your hands."

All hands except little Melvin's went up.

The teacher asked him, "Don't you want to go to Heaven?"

"I heard my father tell my mother 'Business has gone to Hell,'" replied Melvin, "and I want to go where the business went."

Nathan and Ira had been partners for years and now Ira lay dying. Nathan stood at his hospital bedside. "I have a confession to make," said Ira, "I robbed our firm of $100,000. I sold the secret formula to our competitors. I took the letter from your desk that your wife needed to get her divorce. And Nathan, I. . ."

"It's all right," said his partner. "It was me that poisoned you!"

* * *

Business had been terrible for Blum and he cut down on his help. In a month he had to cut down still further, and everyone said that this terrible strain became a fixation that hastened his death a few weeks afterward.

As they were carrying his body down the aisle of the chapel, Blum suddenly sat up in the coffin and asked, "How many men are carrying me?"

"There are eight pallbearers, Mr. Blum," said the undertaker.

"Better lay off two," said Blum lying down again.

Esther Perlmutter, the benevolent Beverly Hills socialite, gets belly laughs with this beaut:

Their ship down, Finkel and Klein were lost on the ocean, clinging to a life raft. Both were pretty tired when suddenly Klein saw a vessel and shouted, "A sail, a sail!"

"So what?" answered Finkel. "We ain't got any samples."

"... and we ain't got any samples!"

Rosenfeld had a thriving dry goods and clothing business. However, the prosperity was too good to last. A competitor moved in on his left and another on his right. One day the rival on the right erected a huge sign that said:

WE HAVE MADE A TERRIBLE MISTAKE
MUST VACATE
HIGHEST VALUE CLOTHING
AT LOWEST PRICES

A few hours later the competitor on Rosenfeld's left, not to be outdone, also put up a banner:

BANKRUPT SALE—CLOSING OUT
AT LESS THAN COST

Before the business day was over, Rosenfeld handled the opposition by putting this sign over his shop:

MAIN ENTRANCE
TO
THE BIG SALE

Customer: Is this suit all wool?
Edelman: I won't lie to you. It's not. The buttons are made of silk.

*   *   *

Cantrowitz and Berkman were discussing their bosses. "My boss," said Cantrowitz, "is such a cheapskate, he should only drop dead!"

"My boss is different," smiled Berkman. "You just can't help liking him. 'Cause if you don't he fires you!"

*   *   *

"I can't understand why you failed in business."

"Too much advertising."

"You never spent a cent in your life on advertising."

"That's true, but my competitor did."

*   *   *

Customer: If that coat cost you $50 how can you afford to sell it to me for $30?
Shenberg: Sh-h-h, my friend. I sell a lot of coats. That's how I can do it!

Shirley Saltzman, the lovely Manhattan homemaker, heard this howler from her accounting whiz hubby, Paul:

Marvin: You and I use the same call girl and I happen to know she charges you, a bookkeeper, twice as much as me. Don't you object?

Barney: Why should I? I use the double entry system.

* * *

Lerner owned a store that had recently been burglarized. He met Fishman, a friend, on the street.

"I am sorry to hear about the robbery," said Fishman. "Did you lose much?"

"Some," replied the storekeeper. "But it would've been a lot worse if the burglar had broken in the night before."

"Why?" asked the friend.

"Well, you see," said Lerner, "just the day of the robbery I marked everything down 20 percent."

Feinstein, the dress manufacturer, kept a goldfish in a bowl on his desk. One day his sales manager noticed it. "What's that for?"

"It's nice, replied Feinstein, "to have something around that opens their mouth without asking for a raise."

* * *

WINDOW SIGN IN KORNFELD'S CLOTHING STORE
USE OUR EASY CREDIT PLAN: 100
PERCENT DOWN
NOTHING TO PAY EACH MONTH!

* * *

Plotkin and Singer, two garment manufacturers, met on Seventh Avenue.

"Good morning!" offered Plotkin.

"Don't talk to me," replied Singer. "You're so crooked that the wool you've been pulling over my eyes is 50 percent polyester."

Benny Wildman, the New Jersey men's clothing mogul, manufactured this rollicking mirthful:

Finkelstein was frantic. For five weeks he hadn't been able to do any business because he'd forgotten the combination to the safe.

Rifkin, his partner, had gone to the Catskills for a vacation and there was no word from him. Then one day the phone rang.

"Thank God you called," Finkelstein shouted into the phone. "I can't do any business. I had to lay off the whole shop, fire the salesmen, refuse orders from our biggest accounts, and just stay here in the office and wait for your call."

"What happened?" asked Rifkin.

"It's the safe. I forgot the combination."

"But it's so simple. Turn once left and twice right."

"But what about the numbers?"

"It doesn't matter," answered Rifkin. "The lock's broken."

"The lock's broken!"

145

Mendelbaum had worked a lifetime without ever taking time off.

The doctor suggested he take his first vacation in Palm Beach. Mendelbaum, carrying a large bucket, walked up to the lifeguard.

"How much would it cost for a pail of salt water?" he asked. "I want to take a little sponge bath back at the motel!"

"A dollar a bucket," said the guard, collecting the money from his easy mark.

The next morning, bucket in hand, Mendelbaum showed up again, but now the tide was out about 800 feet. "Hey, lifesaver!" said Mendelbaum. "You certainly are doing a big business!"

* * *

Fliegelman, a big manufacturer of ladies' dresses in New York, received word that his top traveling salesman had died of a heart attack in a Dallas hotel.

Fliegelman, sent this telegram—collect:

RETURN SAMPLES BY FREIGHT AND
SEARCH HIS PANTS FOR ORDERS.

Margolis was selling his bosom buddy a suit. "I'm telling you, Manny," he said, "that even your best friend won't recognize you in that suit! Just take a walk outside for a minute and get the feel of it."

Manny went out and returned a moment later. Margolis rushed up to him.

"Good morning, stranger," he beamed. "What can I do for you?"

* * *

Rafferty went to Cooperman's Clothing Store to buy a new suit for a wedding.

"You look like a real gentleman," said Cooperman. "Why don't you let me make you a special suit to order?"

"I don't think so," said the Irishman.

"Just tell me what kind of material you like. I'll write to England. They'll get the wool, then they'll weave the cloth, they'll ship it over. I make a pattern, you'll come in for two or three fittings and the suit'll be gorgeous!"

"But I need the suit in three days."

"Don't worry! You'll have it!"

Hornstein manufactured coats but business was so bad the poor man couldn't sleep.

"Count sheep," advised Slodnick, his friend. "It's the best-known cure."

"What can I lose?" signed Hornstein. "I'll try tonight."

The next morning he looked more bleary-eyed than ever. "What happened?" asked Slodnick.

"Sheep I should count," moaned Hornstein. "I counted up to 50,000. Then I sheared the sheep, and made up 50,000 overcoats. Then came the problem that kept me awake all the rest of the night: Where could I get 50,000 linings?"

* * *

A train in Arizona was boarded by robbers, who went through the pockets of the luckless passengers. Greenblatt, a traveling salesman from New York, pulled out $200, but quickly took $4 from the pile and placed it in his vest pocket.

"What'd you do that for?" asked the holdup man, waving his revolver.

"My friend," replied the salesman, "cer-

tainly you wouldn't refuse me 2 percent
discount on a strictly cash transaction like
this?"

* * *

Dugan, a delivery man from near Hy-
annisport making his first trip to New
York, saw the sign CLIMB ONE FLIGHT AND
SAVE $40 ON A NEW SUIT. The Irishman
climbed and immediately was shown a
number of shoddy garments by Spiegal,
the eager salesman. Dugan refused to bite.

Spiegal knew that Zimmer, the boss,
was watching him, so he made a special
effort with the next number. Spiegal
whirled the customer around and around
before the mirror, crying, "It fits like a
glove! You look like a movie star!"

When the Irishman again said "No,"
Zimmer took over, produced one blue serge
suit, and made the sale in 5 minutes. As
Dugan left, the boss said, "You see how
easy it is when you know how? He went
for the first suit I showed him."

"Yeah," agreed Spiegal, "but who made
him dizzy?"

Edwin Lehman, Ship 'n Shore's dashing West Coast manager, delivers this delightful dash of drollery:

A sign in a Brooklyn candy store read: CIGARETTES 60 CENTS A PACKAGE. By 8:00 in the morning a line had already formed all around the block. Markowitz pushed his way to the front of the line.

Polowski, a big burly steelworker grabbed him and shouted, "Get to the rear of the line."

A few minutes later, Markowitz pushed his way through the crowd, got to the door, and the big Polack shoved him away.

Markowitz tried again, and again Polowski shoved him back. Finally, Markowitz said, "Look, if you push me, once more—I ain't gonna open the store!"

"*I ain't gonna open the store!*"

Sussman moved down South into one of the backwater towns and opened a general store. He seemed to be doing well, but then the beginning of April, sales started to slacken.

Sussman tried to figure out why business fell off. He walked down Main Street and discovered that every establishment had an Easter sign out front and that all the windows were especially dressed for the holiday.

Sussman was very religious—he couldn't very well acknowledge Easter. But he did work out the solution. That afternoon, Sussman's general store also had an Easter sign. It said:

CHRIST IS RISEN
BUT SUSSMAN'S PRICES
ARE STILL THE SAME

* * *

Brodsky went to a house of ill repute. He paid $50 and relieved himself. When he finished, Gloria, his bedmate said, "That was great. You're the best I've had in a long time. If you want to go again, it's free."

Brodsky could not turn down such an offer. So he worked himself up, and once again released his pleasure.

When they finished, the girl said, "Mister, you're terrific! I enjoyed that so much that if you want to go again, I'll pay you $50!"

Brodsky rested 15 minutes, but no matter how hard he played with himself, it wouldn't stand up. Finally Brodsky gave up. He grabbed his putz and said, "You son-of-a-bitch bastard. When it comes to spending a buck, you're all there; but when it comes to make a dollar . . . !"

* * *

Customer: What do you mean! Seven hundred dollars for that antique! Last week you only wanted $450.
Schulman: Well, you know how the cost of labor and materials keeps going up.

Grobstein's Clothing Store stood on New York's Lower East Side. One day Grobstein went out for lunch and left Salter, his new salesman, in charge. When he came back Salter proudly announced, "I sold that black cloth coat."

"For how much?" asked Grobstein.

"Ninety-eight cents, like it said on the tag."

"Ninety-eight cents!" screamed the owner. "The tag said 98 *dollars*, you idiot!"

The clerk looked as if he would die of embarrassment. "Let this be a lesson to you!" said Grobstein, "but don't feel bad—we made 10¢ profit."

* * *

JEWISH FOOTBALL YELL

Get that quarter back!

* * *

For 8 days and nights, Schlossberg the suit maker was unable to sleep. No medicine took effect and in desperation, the Schlossberg family brought in a famous hypnotist.

The hypnotist stared at Schlossberg and chanted, "You are asleep, Mr. Schlossberg. The shadows are closing about you. Soft music is lulling you into a state of lovely relaxation. You are asleep! You are asleep!"

"You're a miracle worker," sobbed the grateful son. He gave the hypnotist a big bonus and the man left in triumph.

As the outside door closed, Schlossberg opened one eye. "Say," he demanded, "is that shmuck gone yet?"

* * *

Sam and Irving owned a clothing store. When Sam returned from vacation, he was horrified to find his partner bandaged from head to toe, walking on crutches.

"What happened?" he asked.

"You remember the purple and green checked suit with the narrow lapels we've been stuck with for years?" said Irving. "I sold it!"

"So, what happened to you? The customer didn't like the suit?"

"The customer loved the suit," said Irving, "but the seeing eye dog nearly killed me!"

YOU SHOULD LIVE THAT LONG

Old man Krastenfeld lay on his death-bed for months and finally passed away.

Two weeks later, the relatives gathered like vultures to hear the reading of the will.

The lawyer tore open an envelope, drew out a piece of paper and read:

"Being of sound mind, I spent every dime before I died."

* * *

A Jewish woman in the Bronx recently caused quite a commotion by revealing the contents of her will. First, she stipulated that she be cremated. Then, she asked that her ashes be spread over Bloomingdale's so she'd be assured of having her daughter visit her at least twice a week.

Mrs. Moskowitz loved chicken soup. One evening she was spooning it up when three of her husband's friends came in. "Mrs. Moskowitz," the spokesman said, "we are here to tell you that your husband Izzy has been killed in an automobile accident."

Mrs. Moskowitz continued eating her soup. Again they told her. Still no reaction.

"Look," said the puzzled speaker, "we are telling you that your husband is dead."

She went right on with the soup. "Gentlemen," she said between mouthfuls, "soon as I'm finished with this chicken soup, you gonna hear some scream!"

* * *

Krebs was killed in an accident and Silverman was sent to break the news to his wife.

"Be careful how you tell her," advised a friend. "She's a very delicate woman!"

He knocked on the door and she came out. "Pardon me, are you the widow Krebs?"

"Certainly not."

"You wanna bet?"